Toby's Ark

an around-the-world musical
set on board a Victorian clipper, the Sea Shanty

words by Sue Heaser
music by Alison Hedger

Written for the Southampton Schools' Music Association

Duration approximately 30 minutes

For children aged 4 to 9 years of mixed abilities
also suitable for older children with learning difficulties

Ideal for performance at any time of the year

Involves narration, mime, short dialogue and percussion
Seven new songs, some with actions

TEACHER'S BOOK
Complete with music and script
Production notes and comprehensive supporting educational material included

MUSIC

Song 1.	Sea Shanty (recurs throughout as link music)
Song 2.	It's A Thing-a-me-jig
	(also a What-cha-ma-call and Hoo-ja-ma-flip)
Song 3.	Here Come The Animals
Song 4.	We Are The Children Of Africa
Song 5.	Sing A Song Of Marigolds (India)
Song 6.	Chinese Children Say Hello
Storm Music	
Song 7.	Kinkajou From Peru
Finale Repeat Song 1.	

Matching tape cassette: order No. GA11027
Side A with vocals and side B with vocals omitted

Order No. GA11025

ISBN 0-7119-6003-8

A NOTE FROM 

UNICEF, the United Nations Children's Fund, is the leading agency working for children in over 140 countries. We work with Governments, local people and non-governmental organisations to help them determine the needs of children and provide the basic services that are so essential to their well-being.

Irrespective of nationality or language, UNICEF believes that music can play a special part in the lives of children and young people. For example, at a children's centre in Mozambique, children who have been uprooted and traumatised by many years of war are being helped through a programme called 'Healing through play'. Making music, singing and dancing are some of the ways in which they are learning to mix with other children again and live normal lives once more.

Based on a fun yet informative trip around the world which explores different countries and nationalities in a non-prejudiced way, TOBY'S ARK echoes the beliefs of UNICEF.

If you would like to receive our Education Resources Catalogue or support UNICEF through Music for UNICEF (our 50th Anniversary campaign) or Non-Uniform Day (our annual event for schools) contact:
UNICEF, 55 Lincoln's Inn Fields, London WC2A 3NB. Tel 0171 405 5592

SYNOPSIS

It is 1850 and the clipper ship Sea Shanty is in the port of Southampton (*this may be any 19th century working port*), getting ready for a voyage around the world. A mysterious animal is brought on board in a crate; it was found in the hold of another ship and the crew of the Sea Shanty promise to try to find its home during their voyage. They give it the name 'Thing-a-me-jig'.

A famous explorer, Mr Jungletrotter, has heard that the Sea Shanty is taking the Thing-a-me-jig home. He has brought a collection of animals back from his travels and is now anxious for them to return home. The Sea Shanty's crew agree to take his animals too. Harriet Bloom, a lady scientist who is travelling with the Sea Shanty, promises to look after them on the voyage.

The Sea Shanty sails to Lagos in Nigeria for a cargo of peanuts and delivers back two monkeys, but the African children tell the sailors that the Thing-a-me-jig does not come from their country.

The ship continues on to Calcutta in India where a cargo of jute is loaded and the tigers are delivered home. The Indian children are sorry but the Thing-a-me-jig does not come from their country.

The next port is Shanghai in China. The Sea Shanty loads a cargo of silk and the pandas are delivered home. Once again, the Thing-a-me-jig is found not to belong in China.

The Sea Shanty sails across the Pacific to Paradise Bay in Graham Land, Antarctica, where the penguins joyfully swim ashore. The Thing-a-me-jig shakes its head when asked if it lives there.

Sadly, the ship's crew prepare to return, having failed to find the Thing-a-me-jig's home. A terrible storm blows up as they try to sail round Cape Horn and they are forced to run north before the wind for several weeks. They arrive in an unknown port which they find is Callao in Peru. Peruvian children come to welcome them and at once recognise the Thing-a-me-jig as a little kinkajou – from Peru. There is much rejoicing and lots of kinkajous come flooding onto the ship to welcome the lost kinkajou home. Harriet decides that she will stay on in Peru to follow up the work of Mr Darwin.

Happy that their voyage has been a success, Captain Toby and the crew of the Sea Shanty sail for home.

CAST

Speaking Parts

NARRATOR	this may work best with an adult
SAILORS	one is called Patch
TWO AFRICAN CHILDREN	
TWO INDIAN CHILDREN	
TWO CHINESE CHILDREN	
TWO PERUVIAN CHILDREN	

Mime only (unless you wish to lift speaking parts from the script)

TOBY SALTWATER	captain of the clipper the Sea Shanty
HARRIET BLOOM	a scientist
MR JUNGLETROTTER	an explorer
THING-A-ME-JIG	a tiny kinkajou
MONKEYS	
TIGERS	two of each
PANDAS	
PENGUINS	
EXTRA PENGUINS	for Antarctica
KINKAJOUS	as many as possible
SEA	children in front of the acting area with a length of blue cloth
CHORUS	main body of children sitting facing the audience, divided into four sections: Africa, India, China and Peru. All wear hats they have made to represent their countries in the 19th century.

The Chorus provides singers and percussion players. They follow the story closely at all times and provide an occasional spoken unison line.

PROPS

(*as part of the set*)
- cardboard crate
- ropes and bollards
- ship's wheel
- ship's prow and anchor
- blue fabric

(*other props*)
- Harriet's luggage
- boxes of cargo marked as peanuts, jute and silk
- marigold garlands (golden yellow crepe paper flowers threaded onto a string)
- silver foil fish
- * • honey sandwich
- * • telescope for Toby
- * • Harriet's sketch book

* indicates that these are not essential and may be mimed

LIGHTING

This is not really necessary but could be used to good effect during the storm.

MUSIC AND VOCAL SOUNDS

All the children will probably want to sing all the songs! This is fine and great fun. However, you may choose to reserve certain songs for the part of the Chorus designated as a country. Try to convey the essential mood of each country's song: Africa – strongly rhythmic; India – warm and gentle; China – neat and delicate; Peru – lively and happy.

The instrumental parts are simple and give a great sense of achievement to young players. The parts are best learnt by rote. Using the tape will give speedy results.

Vocal sounds are plentiful. There are animal roars, water splashing and the storm sounds of winds and lashing rain and waves. The children can also emphasise the melody line of the STORM MUSIC. TOBY'S ARK link music provides the perfect piece for youngsters to show off their prowess in whistling!

COSTUMES

TOBY SALTWATER

Toby needs to be dressed as a nineteenth century clipper ship captain with a smart blazer, white or black trousers and a captain's hat.

HARRIET BLOOM

Harriet is modelled on the Victorian lady explorer of which there were several who travelled extensively during the nineteenth century. She should have a long dress and boots, a pith helmet or straw hat tied on with a veil and a parasol. During the voyage, she needs a sketch book in which to draw flowers and animals (see props list*).

MR JUNGLETROTTER

An intrepid Victorian traveller. He could wear a pith helmet, a khaki safari suit and carry a bamboo cane.

SAILORS

Dark trousers or jeans with striped T-shirts or open-necked shirts make easy costumes. Red handkerchiefs round their necks and peaked cloth caps complete the look. Nineteenth century sailors did not usually wear a uniform so the costumes can be varied and colourful.

THE ANIMALS

Monkeys:

Brown hood with ears at the sides, brown tights and jumper. A long wired tail fixed to the waist at the back. Black make-up on the nose.

Tigers:

Yellow or beige jumpers and tights can have black stripes painted on them. A stripy hood with tiger ears. Striped tail as for the monkeys. White socks on the hands and feet for paws with marked claws. Make-up on the face.

Pandas:

Black jogger trousers. White jumper or T-shirt with added black sleeves. Black socks on hands and feet. White hood with small black ears. Make-up: black nose and eye patches.

Penguins:

Black hood with a yellow peak for a beak. Eyes painted on side of the hood. A simple robe shape in black and white fabric adapted as shown in the sketch makes the main costume. Yellow rubber gloves on the feet work well.

The Thing-a-me-jig (and other kinkajous):

A kinkajou is a charming, furry animal from South America resembling a little bear with a long tail. It has a beautiful chestnut coat and large brown eyes. The Thing-a-me-jig is best taken by a fairly small child to provide a contrast between the fearful roars when it is concealed and its emergence as a cuddly little animal. The costume can be made in a similar way to the monkeys' but with the ears more on top of the head. Brown socks for paws. The additional kinkajous that enter at the end can simply have ears on a headband, blackened noses and a tail, to avoid costuming many children.

MONKEY
TIGER
PANDA
gather bottom
edge
PENGUIN
KINKAJOU

TWO SPEAKING CHILDREN FROM EACH COUNTRY

NIGERIAN CHILDREN

T-shirt and shorts or skirt. Sandals. Bright fabric wound round the shoulders. White pill box type hat for the boys (typically Nigerian). Girls should have their hair tied up in a bright scarf and wear lots of beads and bobble earrings.

NIGERIAN

INDIAN CHILDREN

Boys wear a white shirt and a length of sheeting wrapped round them over shorts. Grey or white Nehru-style hat or bare head. Girls wear a T-shirt and skirt, then a length of brightly coloured fabric wrapped round the waist and up over the head to make a simple sari. Alternatively, a long skirt and a length of thin fabric over the head.

INDIAN

CHINESE CHILDREN

Both boys and girls wear trousers (preferably dark
blue) and an anorak or jacket done up at the neck.
Cardboard coolie hat.

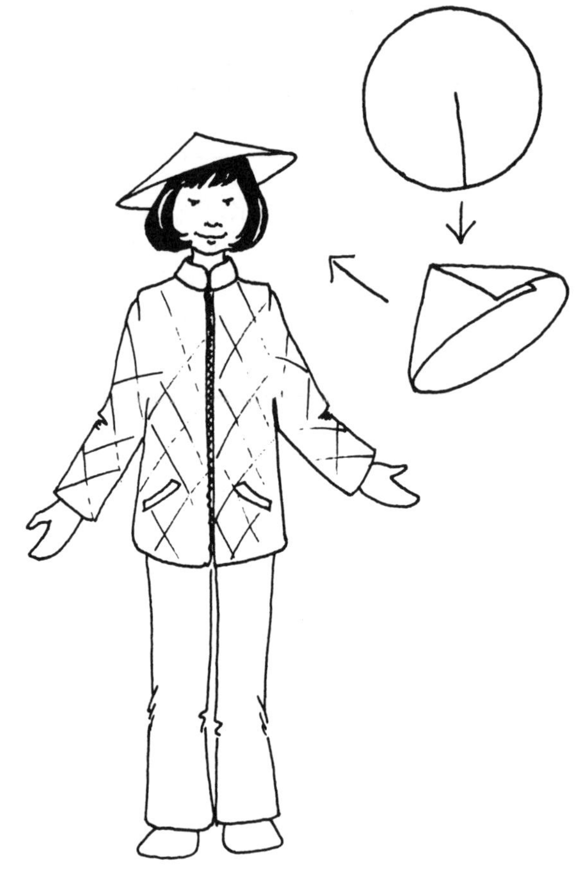

PERUVIAN CHILDREN

A poncho over ordinary clothes. The poncho
can be made from an old blanket with a central
slit for the neck and a fringe added. A woolly
hat with ear flaps.

HATS FOR THE CHORUS

AFRICAN

Boys: White pill box hat made from cardboard.

Girls: Bright scarf tied up and stitched over a beret or wool hat.

INDIAN

Boys: Men's headwear in India is very varied and often depends upon the religion of the wearer. A simple Nehru-style hat in white could be worn. This is like a pill box hat but is pointed back and front, as shown on page 7.

Girls: A length of thin, bright fabric that is simply draped over the head.

CHINESE

Boys and Girls: Cardboard coolie hats. Make these from a large circle of card, cut and stapled as shown in the sketch. A piece of elastic under the chin makes them easier to keep on.

PERUVIAN

Boys and Girls: Woolly hats of all colours and patterns, with or without pompoms. Fabric ear flaps will make them look more authentic.

THE SET

The musical is set on the main deck of the Sea Shanty, a sailing ship of the 1850's. The accompanying sketch shows a suggested layout for the acting area and positioning of the "countries" within the Chorus.

— The suggestion of a mast and sails can be made using a netball post with battens and pieces of sheeting.

— A ship's wheel is needed centre stage for Captain Toby to steer when the ship is at sea. This can be cut out of hardboard and mounted on a simple stand.

— A low ship's prow made of cardboard should be positioned centre front. This can be fixed to a cardboard box to hold it upright.

— A cardboard or hardboard cut-out anchor needs to hang from the prow where it can be lowered into the "sea".

— The bollards can be made from short logs of wood standing on end. Two should be on the "deck" at the front of the acting area and two beyond the blue fabric "sea" to represent a quay. Two ropes with ready-tied loops in their ends tie the ship up. When the Narrator calls "Untie the warps", the sailors remove the loops from the quay bollards and bring them on deck. They reverse the procedure to tie the ship up.

— Two long lengths of blue fabric, to represent the sea, are held at each end by children sitting on the floor round the front of the acting area. When the ship is under way, the fabric is waved to simulate the moving sea. When the sea is stormy, the fabric is shaken vigorously.

— The Thing-a-me-jig's crate is a large cardboard box marked "Dangerous Animal", "Beware" etc. It is positioned to one side of the acting area and can be moved back by the sailors after the Thing-a-me-jig has emerged. The Thing-a-me-jig needs to be hidden inside the box before the start of the musical. The rear of the box away from the audience can be open and Harriet can mime opening the back of the "crate".

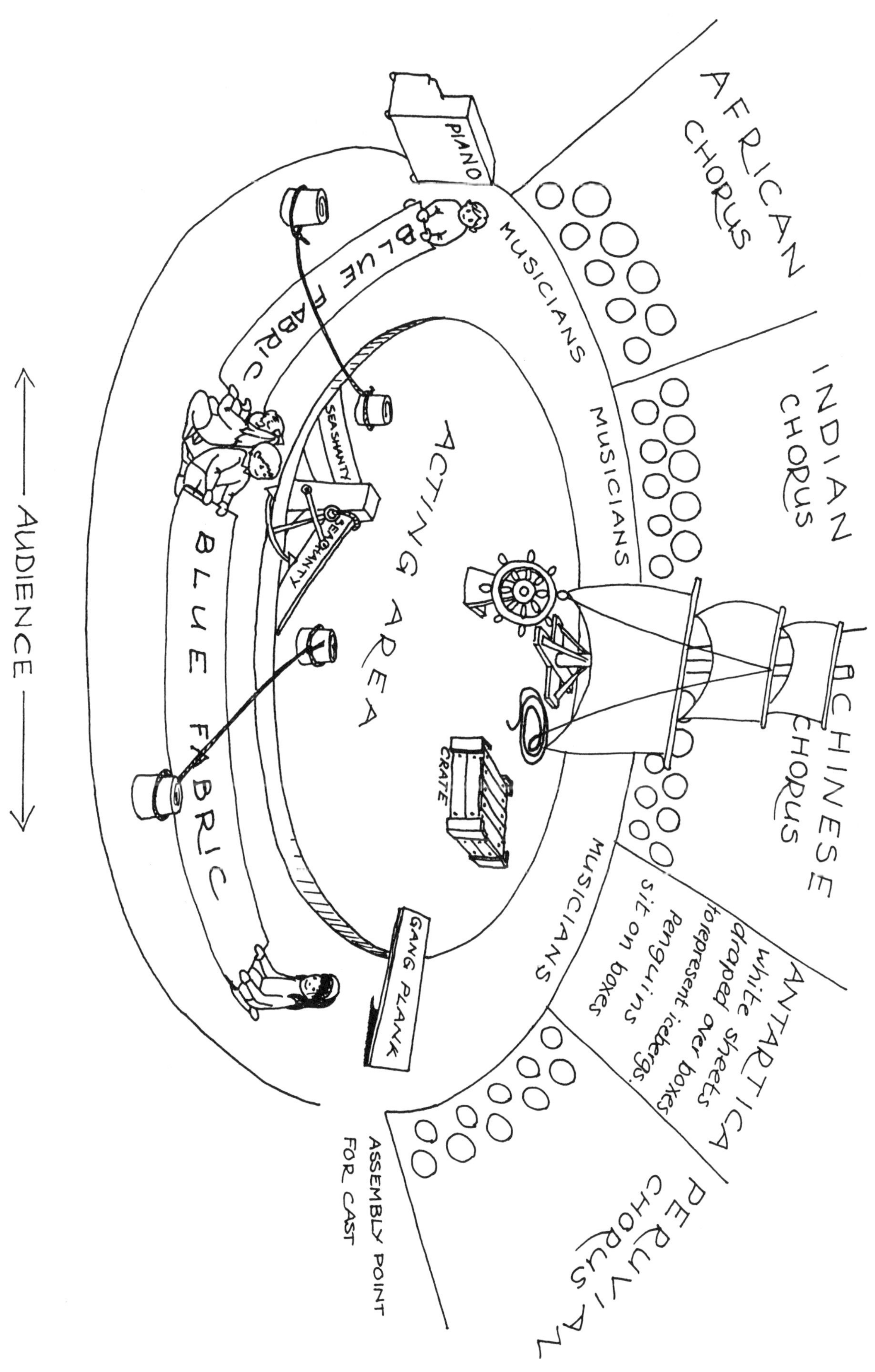

PIANO
AFRICAN CHORUS
INDIAN CHORUS
MUSICIANS
MUSICIANS
BLUE FABRIC
BLUE FABRIC
SEASHANTY
SEASHANTY
ACTING AREA
AUDIENCE
CHINESE CHORUS
CRATE
MUSICIANS
GANG PLANK
ANTARTICA
white sheets draped over boxes to represent icebergs. penguins sit on boxes
PERUVIAN CHORUS
ASSEMBLY POINT FOR CAST

ADDITIONAL SUPPORTING MATERIAL (see also page 56)

THE VOYAGE OF THE SEA SHANTY

The Sea Shanty sets sail from SOUTHAMPTON (*or any local 19th century working port*) and sails south down the Atlantic coast of Europe. The ship passes Gibraltar and continues on down the coast of Africa to reach Lagos in Nigeria where the monkeys are set ashore.

The next leg of the voyage takes the ship around the Cape of Good Hope and up the Indian Ocean and Bay of Bengal to Calcutta in India. Here the tigers are delivered home.

The voyage continues across the Bay of Bengal, through the Strait of Malacca, past Singapore and up the South China Sea to Shanghai in China. The bamboo forests of south-west China are the home of the giant panda but are not found on the coast, so the Chinese children would have had to journey inland with the pandas to take them home.

The Sea Shanty now has to cross the great Pacific Ocean to reach Antarctica, passing many oceanic islands. By now it is summer in the southern hemisphere, the only time that ships can reach Antarctica when it is not ice-bound. The easiest place to reach Antarctica is at the southern end of South America as it is here that the great frozen continent reaches up furthest north. This is also a massive breeding ground for penguins. The ship anchors in Paradise Bay in Graham Land, Antarctica.

They attempt to return home by sailing round Cape Horn where some of the worst seas and weather in the world are found. This is where they encounter the storm which blows the ship north along the west coast of South America, all the way to Callao in Peru, the home of the kinkajou.

See page 14 for historical information on the ports visited

CLIPPER SHIPS
Sailing ships remained largely unchanged in design for three hundred years after the time of Columbus' voyages. Then clipper ships were developed during the 19th century, providing a remarkable advance in speed and sea-worthiness. They soon broke all speed records.

Clippers were long and slender with a very pointed bow, three masts and square-rigged sails. They were ideally suited for long distance trade voyages such as those from Britain to India and the United States to China. However, their reign of supremacy over the seas was short-lived as the age of steam soon arrived and these beautiful ships faded into history.

The Cutty Sark at Greenwich is one of the few remaining clippers that can be seen today.

NAVIGATION
In the 19th century, before electronic navigation was available, ships had to navigate using compass and sextant. The compass showed the ships which way to steer and the sextant helped them to calculate their latitude and longitude on the earth's surface.

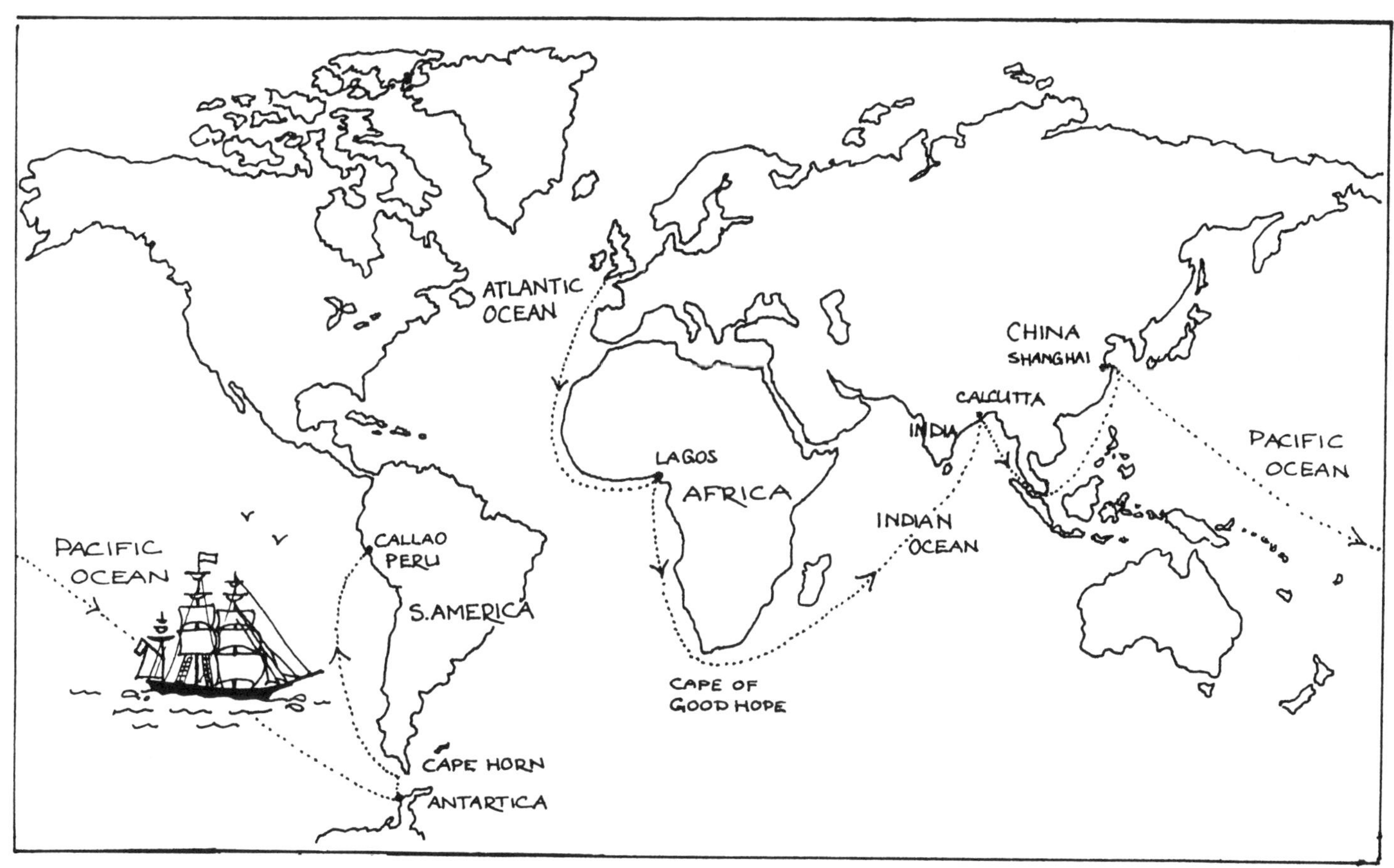

Callao in Peru, is the port for Lima

LIFE ON A 19th CENTURY SHIP

A sailor's life was a hard one. Once a ship had left its home port, it was often many months and sometimes several years before the sailors saw their homes again.

Each ship was like a complete small world and had to be self sufficient for months at a time. A typical clipper ship would have had a captain, a set of officers who carried out the captain's orders, the crew who manned the ship and various craftsmen to keep the ship in good repair, such as a carpenter and a sailmaker. Also on board would have been a cook and sometimes a doctor, and even a ship's artist if the ship was on an exploration.

Food was rationed and often monotonous, consisting of salt beef and ship's biscuits (which often contained weevils!). By the 19th century, many ships carried lime juice or orange juice to help prevent the sailors from getting scurvy. This disease was caused by a lack of fresh vegetables on long voyages. The lime juice gave the British sailors the nickname "Limeys".

SEA SHANTIES

Sea shanties were working songs for sailors on sailing ships. There were many tasks on board these ships that required the men to pull ropes together and the sea shanties were simply a way of helping the men to pull in unison and to encourage them in a laborious task. There were different shanties for the different types of work. For example, capstan shanties were for winding the capstan and halyard shanties were for hauling the halyards. Many ships had a "Shanty man" who would sing a line on his own, then all the sailors would sing an answering chorus while they pulled the ropes.

PORTS IN THE LAST CENTURY

LAGOS, NIGERIA.

Lagos was built on the site of an old Yoruba settlement on an island in the Niger delta. It was named by the Portuguese in 1472 and became a centre for the slave trade. It was annexed by the British in 1861 who abolished the slave trade.

CALCUTTA, INDIA.

Calcutta was founded in 1690 as a trading port of the British East India Company. From 1772 to 1912 Calcutta was the capital of British India, during which time it developed as a busy port and industrial centre. Jute is still a major export.

SHANGHAI, CHINA.

Shanghai was founded in the 11th century and remained a small fishing village for centuries. In 1842 it was opened to foreign trade and became a centre for the silk trade. It is now the largest city in China and one of the world's biggest ports.

PARADISE BAY, ANTARCTICA.

Antarctica was virtually unknown until 1819–1823 when several expeditions from Britain, America and Russia explored the fringes of the continent and the Antarctic Peninsular. It was not until the 1840's that Antarctica was established as a continent. Paradise Bay is situated on the north west side of Graham Land, the Antarctic Peninsular that projects north towards South America. It is the home of large numbers of penguins and the occasional scientist!

CALLAO, PERU.

Callao was founded by the Spanish in 1537. It developed as one of the most active ports on the western coast of South America. It was frequently raided by British buccaneers and destroyed by an earthquake in 1746. After being rebuilt, it remained a possession of Spain until Peruvian independence in the 1820's. The harbour is one of the safest and largest in South America.

Charles Darwin visited Callao on the HMS Beagle in 1833. He described it as a "filthy, ill-built, small seaport"! He also described the nearby city of Lima as in a "wretched state of decay: the streets are nearly unpaved". Lima is now the thriving capital of Peru.

VICTORIAN LADY EXPLORERS

The Victorians were enthusiastic travellers and explorers. Darwin, Livingstone and Stanley are some of the most famous, but there were also several women who defied the conventions of the Victorian age and travelled extensively. The character of Harriet Bloom is based on these brave women.

MARY KINGSLEY 1862–1900

Travelled extensively in West Africa, making scientific studies. She worked for fairer treatment of the African people by their colonial rulers.

MARIANNE NORTH 1830–1890

Marianne travelled widely with her father as a young girl. After his death, she continued to travel across the world, studying plants and painting a wonderful collection of botanical paintings that are now housed in a special gallery at Kew Gardens.

MARGARET FOUNTAINE 1862–1940

Margaret was the daughter of a Norfolk clergyman. After an unhappy love affair, she left England to travel the world and pursue her interest in butterflies. Her diaries are a fascinating account of an enthusiastic traveller and naturalist.

INFORMATION ON SONGS

SONG 1   **SEA SHANTY**

Explanations of the nautical terms:

Halyards — The vertical ropes that run up the mast. When they are pulled, the sails are hoisted.

Heave the lead — 'The lead' was a piece of lead or a weight tied to the end of a line which was marked in fathoms or six foot lengths. Heaving the lead was the method used to measure the depth of the water. The weight was thrown over the side of the ship and the depth was measured by noting how much line went out before the weight reached the bottom.

Cross the bar — Many harbours and rivers had a sand bank at their entrance and this was called the "bar". It would be important to check the depth as a ship crossed the bar when entering or leaving a harbour, in case the water was too shallow.

Batten the hatches — When storms were expected, wooden covers were nailed over any hatches or openings in the ship's hull to protect them from the sea breaking in.

See also the notes on Sea Shanties on Page 13

SONG 4 – WE ARE THE CHILDREN OF AFRICA

There are many languages in Africa. *Ekaro, Dumelang* and *Jambo* are words of welcome from three different languages:

Dumelang   "Hello" in *Tswana*.
                    Pronounced "Doom-a-lang".

Jambo   "Hello" in *Swahili*.
                    Pronounced "Jam-boh".

Ekaro   "Good morning" in *Yoruba*.
                    Pronounced "Ay-car-roh".

SONG 5 – A SONG OF MARIGOLDS (India)

Indian dancing is famous for its graceful hand movements, so here are a few simple ones to accompany the song:

Verse 1:

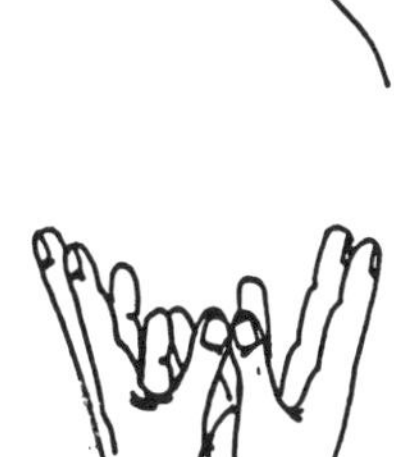

Lines 1 and 2:
Hold hands as in the sketch.
Rotate hands slowly with the music.

Line 3:
Lift arms high, then low.

Line 4:
Cup hands in front of body as shown.
This gesture means "flower" or "marigold".

Refrain : Keeping hands cupped as a marigold,
sway from side to side.

Verse 2:

Lines 1 and 2:
Hold hands as shown and bow slightly.

Line 3:
Indicate a hill.

Line 4:
Indicate a flat plain.

Refrain : As before.

Namashkar is Bengali for "Hello " or "Welcome".

Marigolds are traditionally used in India, made into necklace garlands, to welcome or honour people.

SONG 6 – CHINESE CHILDREN SAY HELLO

Ni Hao?   "How are you?" in Chinese.
Pronounced "nee how".

Tong-zhi   "Friends" or "comrade" in Chinese.
Pronounced "tong-jie".

TOBY'S ARK

Narrator   Welcome to our performance of Toby's Ark.

Captain Toby and Sailors are on the deck of the Sea Shanty. A large crate is positioned to the side of the deck area.

SONG 1   SEA SHANTY

All

    1. Our ship goes sailing o'er the sea.
        Heave, sailors, ho!
        Our ship goes sailing o'er the sea,
        Till we come home in time for tea.
        Heave, sailors, ho!
(calling) Pull the halyards, hoist the sails.
        Pull the halyards, hoist the sails.
        Pull the halyards, hoist the sails.
(sing) Heave, sailors, ho!

    2. Heave the lead and cross the bar.
        Heave, sailors, ho!
        Heave the lead and cross the bar.
        This is the life for a jolly tar.
        Heave, sailors, ho!
(calling) Batten the hatches in the gales.
        Batten the hatches in the gales.
        Batten the hatches in the gales.
        Heave, sailors, ho!

During the song the sailors mime coiling ropes, swabbing the deck and generally being busy.

Narrator   It was early summer in the year 1850 and the crew of the sailing ship Sea Shanty were busy preparing for sea. Today they were

(see page 12)*   to sail from *SOUTHAMPTON on a round-the-world voyage. On the deck was a large crate which contained a mysterious animal that had been found in the hold of another ship. Nobody knew where it had come from and the crew of the Sea Shanty had promised to take it with them on their voyage and see if they could find its home.

Loud roars from everyone as the crate heaves about. Everyone is frightened.

SONG 2A   IT'S A THING-A-ME-JIG

All   *1.*   It's a Thing-a-me-jig, it's a Thing-a-me-jig.   } *twice*
A terrifying, mystifying Thing-a-me-jig.
It has an awful growl.
It has a fearful scowl.
We're very scared when it begins to howl.
It's a Thing-a-me-jig, it's a Thing-a-me-jig.
A terrifying, mystifying Thing-a-me-jig.

Narrator   Just at that moment, a lady came up the gangway.

Enter Harriet Bloom with her luggage. She goes up to Captain Toby and shakes his hand.

She said that her name was Harriet Bloom and she had booked a round-the-world passage on board the Sea Shanty. She was a scientist and wanted to study and sketch the plants and animals that live in different countries. Captain Toby welcomed her onto his ship. Then suddenly . . .

Loud roars from everyone as the crate heaves about.

As soon as Harriet Bloom heard the story of the Thing-a-me-jig she asked if they could let the creature out.

Sailors look scared and draw back, shaking their heads.

But nobody dared. So Harriet shrugged her shoulders and opened the crate. But nothing happened. The Thing-a-me-jig did not seem to want to come out. So Harriet told Patch, one of the sailors, to offer it his honey sandwich which he was eating.

Patch nervously edges forward. There is a pause, then a tiny furry creature emerges, takes the sandwich and eats it greedily. The sailors all relax.

Narrator   What a funny little furry darling Thing-a-me-jig!

SONG 2B   IT'S A THING-A-ME-JIG

All   It's a Thing-a-me-jig, it's a Thing-a-me-jig.   } *twice*
A funny little furry darling Thing-a-me-jig.
It's got a snubby nose
And curly twirly toes.
But where it comes from nobody knows.
It's a Thing-a-me-jig, it's a Thing-a-me-jig.
A funny little furry darling Thing-a-me-jig.

Narrator　　　　　　　　　Everyone was very relieved that the Thing-a-me-jig was not fierce after all. Harriet said that she would look after it on the voyage.

Harriet takes the Thing-a-me-jig to her side. Enter Mr Jungletrotter.

** could be any
Northern hemisphere
seafaring country*

At that moment a man came up the gangway and asked to speak to the Captain. He said that he was Mr Jungletrotter, the famous explorer. On his last world expedition he had brought some animals back to *ENGLAND from the different countries he had visited. He had thought that the people of *ENGLAND would be interested to see them. But the animals had become more and more unhappy away from their homes and he was now very anxious to return them to their own countries. He had heard that the Sea Shanty was already taking another animal home; could they take his too? Everyone said . . .

All　　　　　　　　　　Of course we will!

SONG 3　　　　　HERE COME THE ANIMALS

At each verse the respective animals board the ship and settle down.

Mr Jungletrotter boards the ship along with his animals, and continues to remain on board, turning his hand to being a sailor for the rest of the musical.

All

1.　Here come the animals onto the ship,
Onto the ship, onto the ship.
They are so happy to go on this trip.
Here they come onto the ship.

2.　Here come the monkeys all giggle and swing,
Giggle and swing, giggle and swing.
They are so happy to go on this trip.
Here they come onto the ship.

3.　Here come the tigers all stripy and proud,
Stripy and proud, stripy and proud.
They are so happy to go on this trip.
Here they come into the ship.

4.　Here come the pandas all bumble and thump,
Bumble and thump, bumble and thump.
They are so happy to go on this trip.
Here they come onto the ship.

5.　Here come the penguins all paddly flip,
Paddly flip, paddly flip.
They are so happy to go on this trip.
Here they come onto the ship.

Narrator	Soon it was time to set sail. Captain Toby gave his orders. "All hands on deck."

Sailors   Aye aye!

Narrator   "Untie the warps."

Sailors   Aye aye!

Narrator   "Hoist the mainsail."

Sailors   Aye aye!

LINK MUSIC from SONG 1

Captain Toby takes the wheel. The fabric is waved at the front of the acting area for the moving sea, and continues until "Tie up the ship".

Narrator   And so the good ship Sea Shanty sailed off across the ocean. At first it was very cold and all the animals shivered and shook. (*Everybody does*) Then, as the ship made its way further south it became much hotter. (*All start wiping their brows and fanning themselves*) At last they arrived in Lagos on the coast of Africa where the monkeys lived. Land ho! (*All point excitedly to the African section of the Chorus who stand*) "Tie up the ship." said Captain Toby.

Sailors   Aye aye!

Two African Children *enter saying* . . .

     We are the children of Africa.

SONG 4   WE ARE THE CHILDREN OF AFRICA

African Chorus or All

1. We are the children of Africa.
Dumelang, dumelang, jambo-ha. } *4 times*

2. Ekaro, ekaro to Africa.   *4 times*

Both parts of the song are then sung simultaneously after a short musical link, as follows:

Verse 1. *4 times*   Verse 2. *8 times*

(It is a good idea if the children use their fingers to count off how many times they have sung their part. The music trails away, finishing quietly.)

| **Narrator** | The monkeys left the ship and were greeted joyfully by the African children who promised to take them back to their jungle. (*Harriet brings the Thing-a-me-jig forward*) "Before you go, please can you tell us if this creature is one of yours?" |

| **Two African Children** | What is it called? |

| **Narrator** | It's a Thing-a-me-jig . . . or perhaps it's a What-cha-ma-call! |

SONG 2C   IT'S A WHAT-CHA-MA-CALL

All

It's a What-cha-ma-call, it's a What-cha-ma-call,   } *twice*
A funny little furry darling What-cha-ma-call.
It's got a longish tail
And such a mournful wail,
We have to find its home we must not fail.
It's a What-cha-ma-call, it's a What-cha-ma-call,
A funny little furry darling What-cha-ma-call.

All the African children gaze at the Thing-a-me-jig and shake their heads.

Narrator — The African children said they were very sorry but the Thing-a-me-jig did not live in their country. Harriet took the Thing-a-me-jig back on board. The Sea Shanty spent a happy week in Lagos. The sailors loaded their cargo of peanuts and Harriet painted many of the plants and animals of Africa. At last it was time to set sail again. "Untie the warps."

(The African Chorus sits)

Sailors — Aye aye!

Narrator — "Hoist the mainsail."

Sailors — Aye aye!

LINK MUSIC from SONG 1

The material sea is waved and continues until "Tie up the ship".

Narrator — The Sea Shanty had to sail all round the bottom of Africa and up through the Indian Ocean. It got very hot indeed. Then the wind blew hard and the sea got rather rough. All the animals were sea sick. (*They mime holding their tummies and groan*) At last they arrived in Calcutta on the coast of India, which was the home of the tigers. Land ho! (*All excitedly point to the Indian section of the Chorus who stand*) "Tie up the ship." said Captain Toby.

Sailors   Aye aye!

Enter two Indian children who garland the sailors with marigolds.

SONG 5   SING A SONG OF MARIGOLDS (India)

See page 17 for hand actions

Indian Chorus   *1.*   Sing a song of India,
or All   Sing a song of India.
                                 Sing it high and sing it low.
                                 Sing a song of marigolds.
                                 Marigolds, marigolds.
                                 Sing a song of marigolds.

                 2.   Namashkar to India,
                                 Land of many people.
                                 Some are people of the hills,
                                 Some are people of the plains.
                                 Marigolds, marigolds.
                                 Sing a song of marigolds.

       repeat verse 1.   Sing a song of India . . .

Narrator   The tigers left the ship and were greeted joyfully by the Indian children who promised to take them back to their jungle. (*Harriet brings the Thing-a-me-jig forward*) "Before you go, please can you tell us if this creature is one of yours?"

Two Indian Children What is it called?

Narrator   It's a Thing-a-me-jig . . . or perhaps it's a Hoo-ja-ma-flip!

SONG 2D   IT'S A HOO-JA-MA-FLIP

All   It's a Hoo-ja-ma-flip, it's a Hoo-ja-ma-flip.   }
                         A funny little furry darling Hoo-ja-ma-flip.   }   *twice*
                         It has such big brown eyes
                         Which make us realise,
                         That all of us must sadly sympathise.
                         It's a Hoo-ja-ma-flip, it's a Hoo-ja-ma-flip.
                         A funny little furry darling Hoo-ja-ma-flip.

All the Indian children gaze at the Thing-a-me-jig and shake their heads.

Narrator The Indian children said they were very sorry but the creature did not live in their country. Harriet took the Thing-a-me-jig back on board. The sailors loaded their cargo of jute while Harriet studied the beautiful plants and animals in India. At last it was time to set sail again. "Untie the warps." said Captain Toby.

(The Indian Chorus sits)

Sailors Aye aye!

Narrator "Hoist the mainsail."

Sailors Aye aye!

LINK MUSIC from SONG 1

The material sea is waved and continues until "Tie up the ship".

Narrator This time the Sea Shanty had to sail further east passing by many large islands. Then at last they arrived in China at the port of Shanghai. This was where the pandas came from. Land ho!

All excitedly point to the Chinese section of the Chorus who stand.

"Tie up the ship." said Captain Toby.

Sailors Aye aye!

Enter two Chinese children.

SONG 6 CHINESE CHILDREN SAY HELLO

Chinese Chorus or All

1. Ni Hao? Ni Hao?
    We welcome you.
    Chinese children say hello.
    Ni Hao too.

Refrain Ni Hao? Ni Hao?
    Ni Hao Tong-zhi?
    Chinese children say hello.
    Friends we shall be.

2. Bring the rice, bring the bowl,
    Bring a bell to ring.
    Almond blossom, cherry blossom
    And a song to sing.

Refrain Ni Hao? Ni Hao? . . .

| **Narrator** | The pandas left the ship and were greeted joyfully by the Chinese children who promised to take them back to their bamboo forest. (*Harriet brings the Thing-a-me-jig forward*) "Before you go, please can you tell us if this creature is one of yours?" |

| **Two Chinese Children** | What is it called? |

| **Narrator** | A Thing-a-me-jig. |

repeat SONG 2B   IT'S A THING-A-ME-JIG

All

It's a Thing-a-me-jig, it's a Thing-a-me-jig.   }
A funny little furry darling Thing-a-me-jig.   }   *twice*
It's got a snubby nose
And curly twirly toes.
But where it comes from nobody knows.
It's a Thing-a-me-jig, it's a Thing-a-me-jig.
A funny little furry darling Thing-a-me-jig.

All the Chinese children gaze at the Thing-a-me-jig and shake their heads.

| **Narrator** | The Chinese children said they were sorry but the Thing-a-me-jig did not live in their country. (*The Thing-a-me-jig returns sadly to Harriet*) The Sea Shanty spent a happy time in Shanghai. The sailors loaded their cargo of silk and Harriet sketched many beautiful plants and animals. At last it was time to set sail again. "Untie the warps." said Captain Toby. |

(The Chinese Chorus sits)

| **Sailors** | Aye aye! |

| **Narrator** | "Hoist the mainsail." |

| **Sailors** | Aye aye! |

LINK MUSIC from SONG 1

The material sea is waved.

| Narrator | Now the Sea Shanty had to sail across the great Pacific Ocean. They saw flying fish that the penguins caught for their supper. (*Penguins squawk and catch some silver foil fish thrown onto the deck*) They crossed the Equator and sailed further and further south. It became colder and colder and everyone shivered and shook (*they do*) until at last they could see the snowy land of Antarctica where the penguins lived. |

All excitedly point to Antarctica where several penguins play on the ice. The sea stops moving.

Narrator	"Let go the anchor."

Sailor	Aye aye!

The sailors gently lower the anchor.

Narrator	No people live in Antarctica but they could see lots of penguins playing on the icebergs. The two penguins were so excited to be back home. One by one they jumped from the ship into the icy waters. (*Penguins jump one by one, to two enormous vocal splashing noises made by everyone*) The penguins swam off towards their friends, waving goodbye. Captain Toby went over to the Thing-a-me-jig and gently patted it on the head. "Now then, little Thing-a-me-jig" he said, "Do you live here?" (*The Thing-a-me-jig sadly shakes its head*) Everyone was very sad. They had been all around the world and still had not found a home for the little Thing-a-me-jig. "What can we do?" asked everyone. "We'll just have to take it back home with us." said Captain Toby. So sadly the crew of the Sea Shanty set off once more. (*Narrator speaks slowly and sadly*) "Haul up the anchor."

Sailors *(sadly)*	Aye aye!

Narrator	"Hoist the mainsail."

Sailors	Aye aye!

LINK MUSIC from SONG 1, *this time sadly.*

The material sea is waved, gently at first, and continues until the ship is tied up.

Narrator	The quickest way home for the Sea Shanty was to sail around Cape Horn, which is one of the stormiest places in the world. Captain Toby felt anxious about such a difficult voyage but they all hoped that they would be lucky and miss the worst storms. Then, just as they had nearly reached the Cape . . .

Everyone very quietly begins to make the vocal sound of the wind. This continues quietly as the Narrator speaks.

Look, look! A terrible storm is coming this way!

All point to the direction of the gathering storm.

All hands on deck! Batten down the hatches!

The wind gets louder and the sea becomes more agitated.

STORM MUSIC

Everyone contributes either with vocal sounds, percussion instruments or singing the melody as the storm rages.

During the music the people on the Sea Shanty run from one side of the acting area to the other to simulate a rolling ship. This is most effective if the children all run to the left and pause, then all run to the right and pause, and so on. They need to tilt their bodies in the direction they are going as though the deck has tipped and they are unable to stop themselves. At end of music all yell and fall to the floor. Blackout if lighting is used. Pause. Lights come up slowly and those in acting area slowly raise their heads and look around.

Narrator   The storm had blown for many days and the Sea Shanty had been forced to turn north and run before the wind. She had travelled many miles off her course. At last they sighted land. (*All point to the Peruvian section of the Chorus who stand*) and a little port appeared in front of them. "Tie up the ship!"

Sailors   Aye aye!

Narrator   Wherever can we be? Listen, what's that sound?
It's like nothing we have heard before.

(**PERUVIAN PIPES PLAY** *– listen to matching tape*).

Two Peruvian Children *enter saying* . . .

Welcome to our country.

Narrator   Where are we?

**Two Peruvian
Children**   This is Callao in Peru.

Narrator
(*extremely surprised*)   Peru!! Everyone was very surprised but also excited. The storm had blown them all the way to Peru. Harriet was delighted; she had heard all about Peru from the famous explorer Mr Charles Darwin!

| **(Narrator** contd.) | "Shall we ask them about the Thing-a-me-jig?" asked Captain Toby. "Yes, let's." everyone replied. (*Harriet brings the Thing-a-me-jig forward*) "Please can you tell us, is this creature one of yours?" |

| **Two Peruvian Children** | Yes! It's a kinkajou! From Peru! |

| **Narrator plus All** | A kinkajou from Peru!! |

SONG 7   KINKAJOU FROM PERU

| **All** | **Kinkajou, kinkajou, kinkajou is from Peru.**
Kinkajou to wink at you.
Kinka-kinka-jou!! | *repeat*
as
required |

With continuing music, as many children as possible dressed as Kinkajous skip and dance around the acting area, up the aisles and around the audience.

| **Narrator** | And so by good fortune the Sea Shanty had found the home of the mysterious Thing-a-me-jig at last. The Peruvian children told them that kinkajous are also called "honey bears" because they love honey. "That's why it liked my honey sandwich" said Patch. Now their voyage was over and they had taken all the animals back to their homes, it was time for the Sea Shanty to go home too. |

Harriet steps up to Captain Toby

Harriet told Captain Toby that she had decided to stay in Peru to study the wonderful plants and animals. She had also become very fond of the little Thing-a-me-jig, the kinkajou. "Will you collect me the next time you pass this way?" she asked. "Of course we will!" everyone shouted. And so the good ship Sea Shanty set sail for home, leaving Harriet in Peru.

Harriet collects her luggage and stands on the shore with the kinkajous and the two Peruvian children.

Narrator	"Untie the warps."
Sailors	Aye aye!
Narrator	"Hoist the mainsail."
Sailors	Aye aye!

Entire Chorus stands and the sea is flapped for the last time!

FINALE repeat   SONG 1 SEA SHANTY

All cast enter the main acting area and wave along with the Chorus at their audience.

THE END

1
SEA SHANTY

All + claps

Opening number and Finale

G C G   C   D   G   G
time for tea.
jol - ly tar.
Heave, sail - ors, ho!
(calling):
Pull the hal - yards,
Bat - ten the hatch - es
f
Am7   D7   G   Em
hoist the sails.
in the gales.
Pull the hal - yards,
Bat - ten the hatch - es
hoist the sails.
in the gales.
Pull the hal - yards,
Bat - ten the hatch - es
simile
To repeat
To finish
Am   D7   G   G
hoist the sails.
in the gales.
(singing):
Heave, sail - ors, ho!
ho!
f
Em   G   D7   G   (claps)
mf

IT'S A THING-A-ME-JIG

All + woodblocks
1. cue: Loud roars as the crate heaves about. Everyone is frightened.
2. cue: What a funny little furry darling Thing-a-me-jig!

(Words for 2a – top line, words for 2b – bottom line)

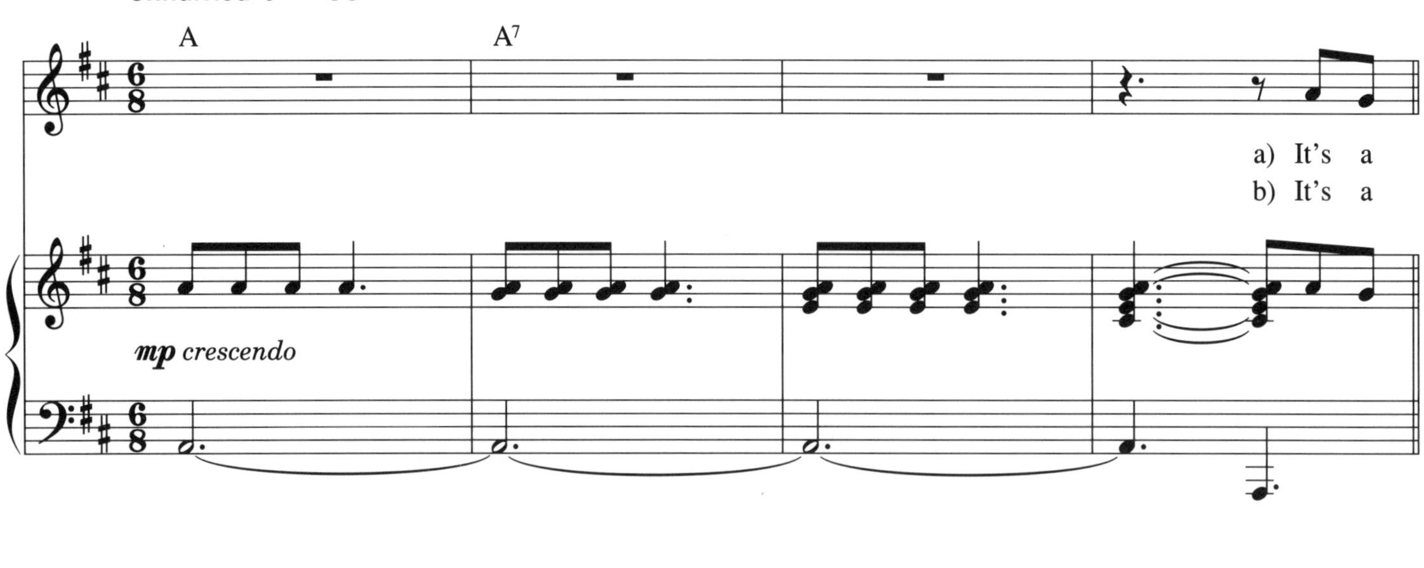

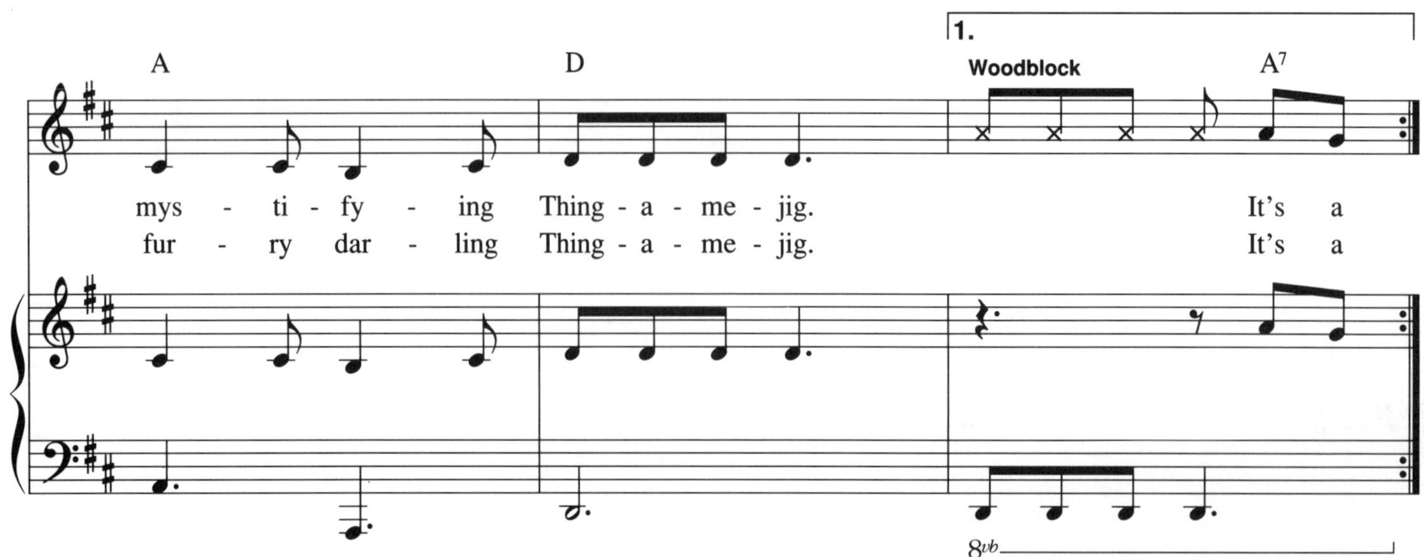

Woodblock
C
D
C
a) It has an aw - ful growl._____ It has a fear - ful
b) It's got a snub - by nose_____ and cur - ly twir - ly
8vb
D
C
F F# G Ab A
scowl._____ We're ve - ry scared when it be - gins to howl.
toes._____ But where it comes from no - bod - y knows.
D
D/C#
Bm
Bm/A
It's a Thing - a - me - jig, it's a Thing - a - me - jig. A
It's a Thing - a - me - jig, it's a Thing - a - me - jig. A
f
G
Em
A
D
Woodblock
ter - ri - fy - ing, mys - ti - fy - ing Thing - a - me jig.
fun - ny lit - tle fur - ry darl - ing Thing - a - me - jig.
f

3
HERE COME THE ANIMALS

All + two glockenspiels
cue: Of course we will!

F
G
C
1.
(2 part glocks play)
Here they come on - to the ship.
G
2.
(2 part glocks play)
G
3.
(2 part glocks play)
G
(on repeat L.H. in octaves to finish)
C
F
C
F
C
4. Here come the pan - das all bum - ble and thump, bum - ble and thump,
5. Here come the pen - guins all pad - dl - y flip, pad - dl - y flip,
mf

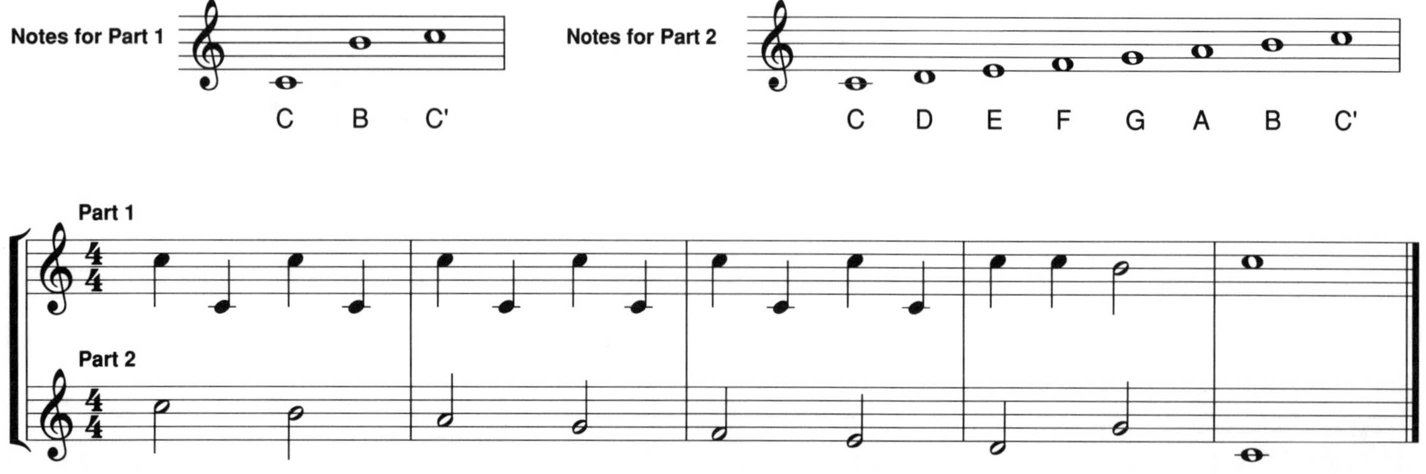

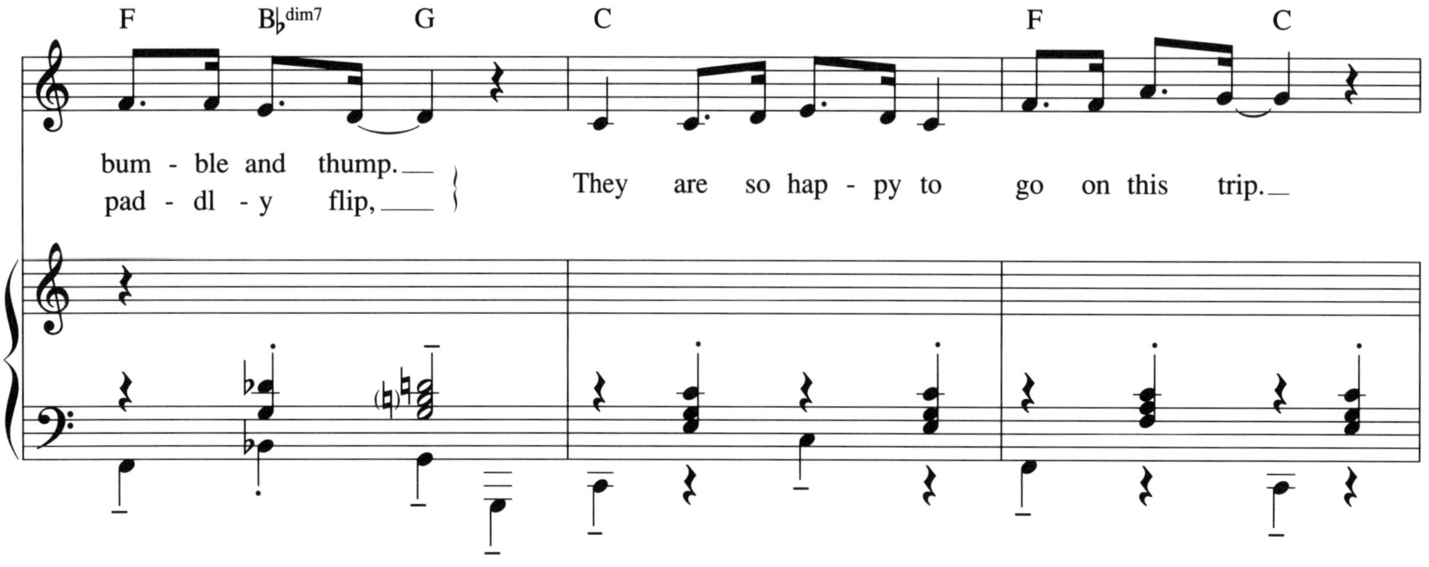
F
B♭dim7
G
C
F
C
bum - ble and thump.
pad - dl - y flip,
They are so hap - py to go on this trip.

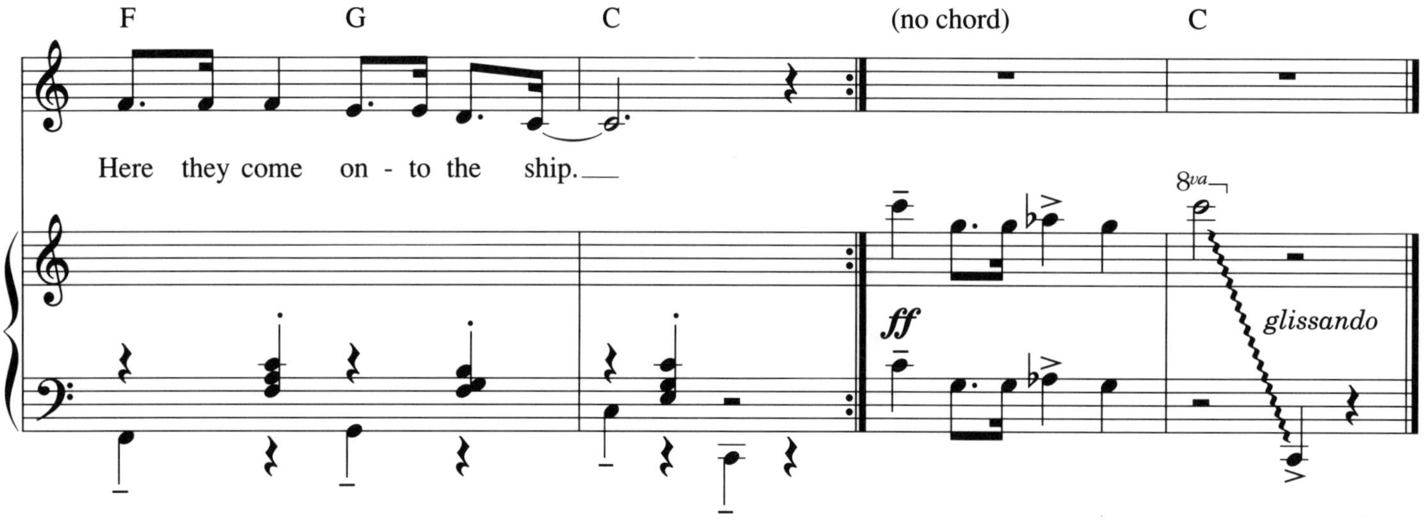
F
G
C
(no chord)
C
Here they come on - to the ship.
8va
ff
glissando

Two-part glockenspiel introduction and link between verses.

Notes for Part 1

C B C'

Notes for Part 2

C D E F G A B C'

Part 1
Part 2

LINK MUSIC from Song 1

whistling or kazoos
cue: Hoist the mainsail. Aye aye!

4
WE ARE THE CHILDREN OF AFRICA

African Chorus + tom-toms
(two part singing)
cue: We are the children of Africa.

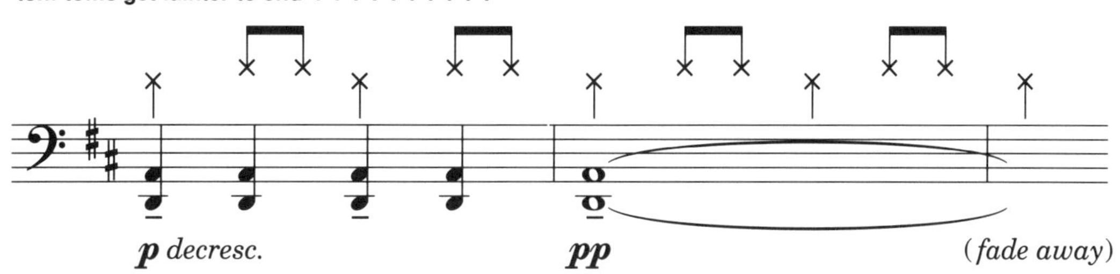

D
G   Em   D
2. E - ka - ro,   e - ka - ro to   Af - ri - ca.
f
C   Em   D
D
E - ka - ro,   e - ka - ro to   Af - ri - ca.
div.
2. E - ka - ro,   e - ka - ro to
1. We   are the   child - ren of
(sing this section 4 times)
ff
G   Em   D
G   Em   D
Af - ri - ca.
(2.) E - ka - ro,   e - ka - ro to   Af - ri - ca.
Af - ri - ca.
Du - me - lang,   du - me - lang,   jam - bo - ha.
(decresc. through 3rd and 4th times)

CODA

tom-toms get fainter to end . . . .
p decresc.
pp
(fade away)

IT'S A WHAT-CHA-MA-CALL

All except African Chorus + woodblocks
cue: It's a Thing-a-me-jig . . . or perhaps it's a What-cha-ma-call!

2.
Woodblock
C
D
C
It's got a long - ish tail and such a mourn - ful
8vb
D
C
F   F#   G   Ab   A
wail. We have to find its home, we must not fail.
D   D/C#   Bm   Bm/A
It's a What - cha - ma - call, it's a What - cha - ma - call. A
f
G   Em   A   D   Woodblock
fun - ny lit - tle fur - ry darl - ing What - cha - ma - call.
f

LINK MUSIC from Song 1

whistling or kazoos
cue: Hoist the mainsail. Aye aye!

5
A SONG OF MARIGOLDS (India)

Indian Chorus + Indian bells* + actions
cue: Tie up the ship said Captain Toby. Aye aye!

* Can be improvised. Ideas are given on matching tape.   **Repeat verse 1. to finish song**

IT'S A HOO-JA-MA-FLIP

All except Indian Chorus + woodblocks
cue: It's a Thing-a-me-jig . . . or perhaps it's a Hoo-ja-ma-flip!

Woodblock
C
D
C
It has such big brown eyes which makes us re - a -
D
C
F F# G Ab A
- lise, that all of us must sad - ly sym - pa - thise.
D
D/C#
Bm
Bm/A
It's a Hoo - ja - ma - flip, it's a Hoo - ja - ma - flip. A
G
Em
A
D
Woodblock
fun - ny lit - tle fur - ry darl - ing Hoo - ja - ma - flip.
f
f
f

LINK MUSIC from Song 1

whistling or kazoos
cue: Hoist the mainsail. Aye aye!

6

CHINESE CHILDREN SAY HELLO

Chinese Chorus + metallophone + gong
cue: Tie up the ship said Captain Toby. Aye aye!

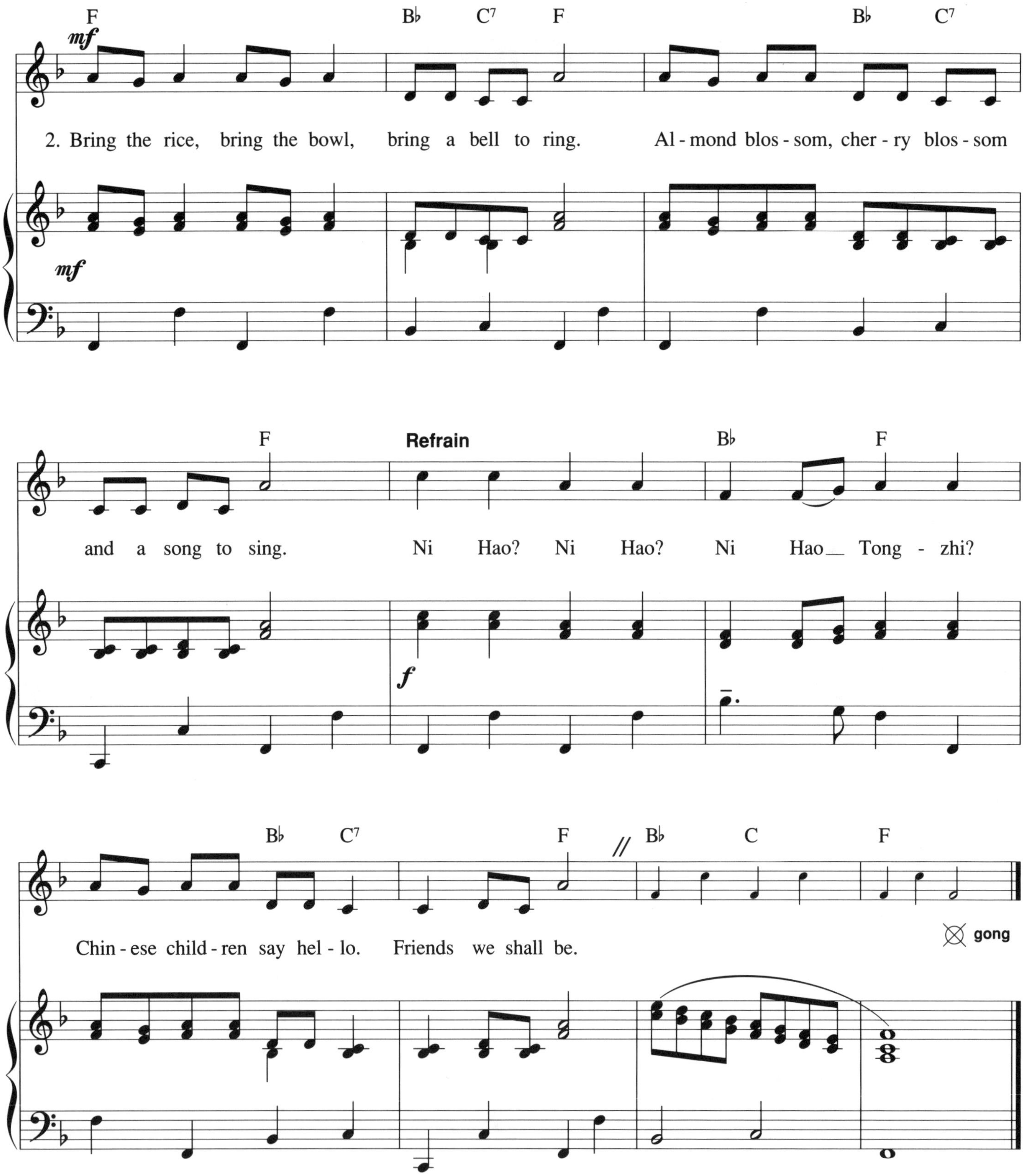

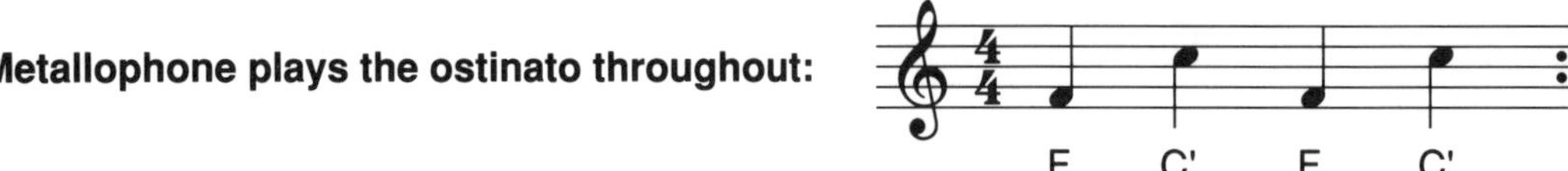

F Bb C7 F Bb C7
mf
2. Bring the rice, bring the bowl, bring a bell to ring. Al - mond blos - som, cher - ry blos - som
F Refrain Bb F
and a song to sing. Ni Hao? Ni Hao? Ni Hao Tong - zhi?
f
Bb C7 F Bb C F
Chin - ese child - ren say hel - lo. Friends we shall be.
gong

Metallophone plays the ostinato throughout:

F C' F C'

IT'S A THING-A-ME-JIG

All except Chinese Chorus + woodblocks
cue: What is it called? A Thing-a-me-jig.

2.
Woodblock
C
D
C
It's got a snub - by nose. and curl - y twirl - y
8vb
D
C
F F# G Ab A
toes. But where it comes from no - bod - y knows.
D
D/C#
Bm
Bm/A
It's a Thing - a - me - jig, it's a Thing - a - me - jig. A
f
G Em A
D
Woodblock
fun - ny lit - tle fur - ry darl - ing Thing - a - me - jig.
f

# LINK MUSIC from Song 1

whistling or kazoos
2 x cue: Hoist the mainsail. Aye aye!

STORM MUSIC

with added percussion + vocal sounds
cue: All hands on deck! Batten down the hatches!

PERUVIAN PIPES PLAY

cue: It's like nothing we have heard before.

Play any random notes, so as to improvise a melody.
(Listen to matching tape)

7
KINKAJOU FROM PERU

Peruvian Chorus + tongue clicks
cue: A kinkajou from Peru!!

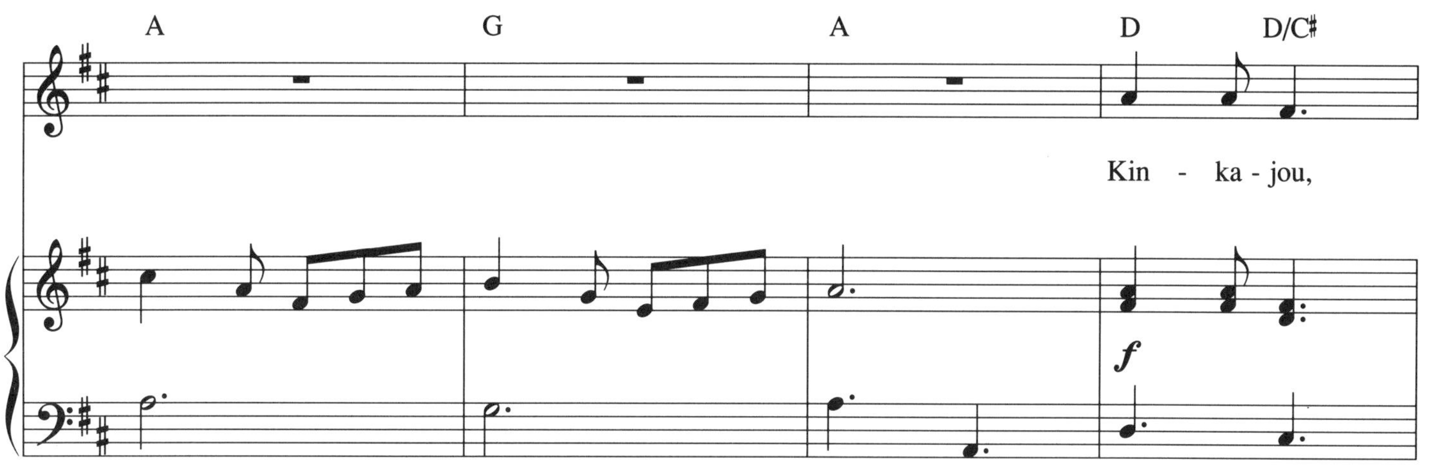

A   G   A   D   D/C#
Kin - ka - jou,
f

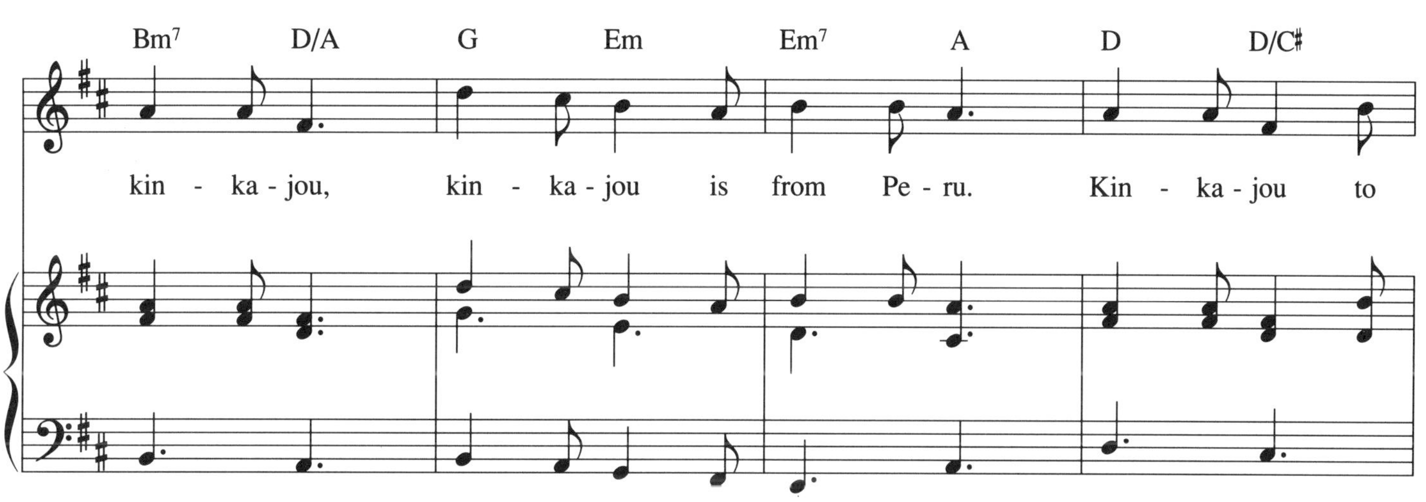

Bm7   D/A   G   Em   Em7   A   D   D/C#
kin - ka - jou, kin - ka - jou is from Pe - ru. Kin - ka - jou to

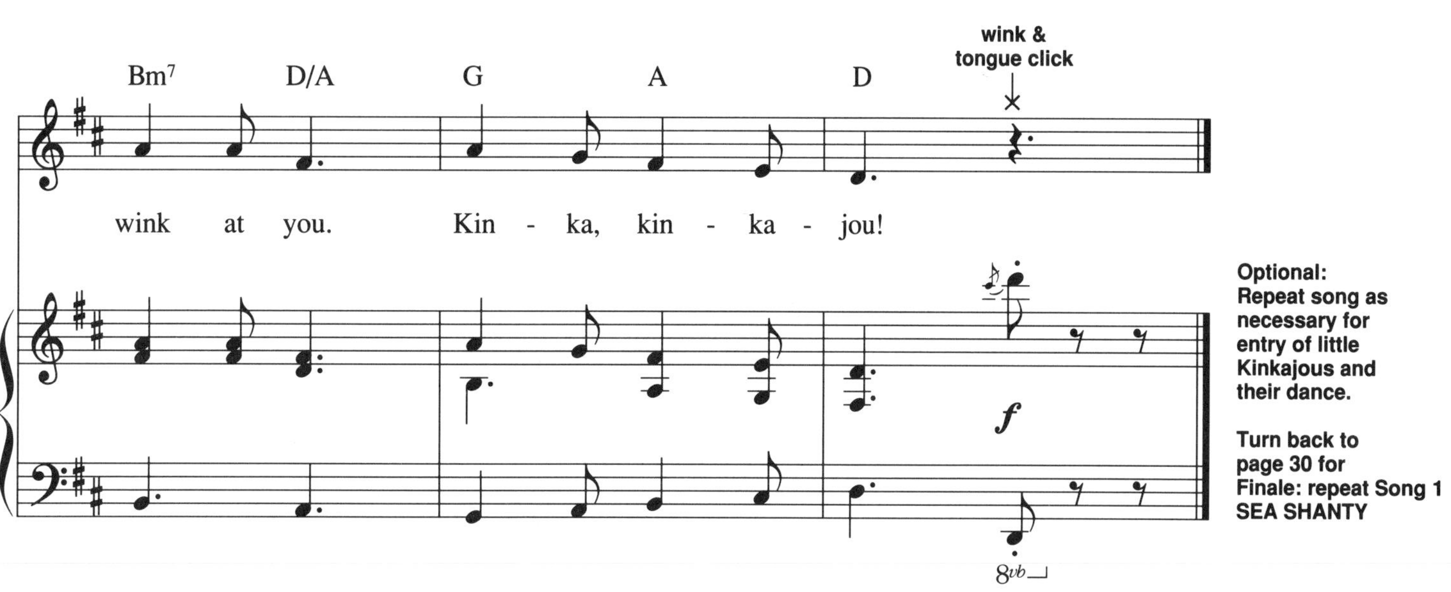

Bm7   D/A   G   A   D
wink & tongue click
wink at you. Kin - ka, kin - ka - jou!
f
8vb

Optional:
Repeat song as
necessary for
entry of little
Kinkajous and
their dance.

Turn back to
page 30 for
Finale: repeat Song 1
SEA SHANTY

THE TELESCOPE

The telescope is a very useful instrument for sailors as it means that they can see distant objects more clearly. It helps them keep a look out for danger; they can spot a dangerous coast when it is still far off; lights flashing at night in the distance can be identified; and they can see other ships more easily to be sure there is no danger of collision.

The telescope was invented in 1608 by a Dutch optician and was modelled after a simple instrument built by Galileo, the famous Italian scientist. In 1609, Galileo began to study the sky with a telescope and discovered that the earth moves around the sun.

THE MICROSCOPE AND CHARLES DARWIN

The microscope was invented in 1590 by Dutch spectacle makers, Hans and Zacharias Janssen. When Darwin returned from his famous voyage on the Beagle in 1836, he brought back many specimens of plants and animals. He soon found that the microscopes available at the time were not strong enough for him to study his specimens properly so he asked a London firm to make him an instrument to suit his needs. This they did and Darwin's studies led to his famous work "On the Origin of Species", published in 1859. In this, he presented his Theory of Evolution which scandalised Victorian society but is still used as the basis for the study of how animals and plants evolved.

THE PANAMA CANAL

The Panama canal is 51 miles (82 km) long and provides a passage for ships between the Carribean Sea and the Pacific Ocean. Until it was built, ships travelling from one coast of North America to the other had to make a journey of nearly 6000 miles (10,000 kms) round the dangerous Cape Horn at the southern most tip of South America.

It was in 1848, during the Californian gold rush, that the first moves were made to get a canal built across the isthmus of Panama. Work was begun in 1878 by a French company but there were many problems and so many men died that the project was abandoned in 1887.

At last, the United States took on the task of finishing the canal and it was opened in 1914.

When the Sea Shanty made her voyage in 1850, the Canal was still only being planned. So Captain Toby had to take his ship home the long way, round Cape Horn.

Printed and bound in Great Britain by
Caligraving Limited Thetford Norfolk